MISS MARY MACK

MISS MARY MACK

AND OTHER
CHILDREN'S STREET RHYMES

COMPILED BY
JOANNA COLE
AND
STEPHANIE CALMENSON

ILLUSTRATED BY
ALAN TIEGREEN

A Beech Tree Paperback Book / New York

Text copyright © 1990 by Joanna Cole and Stephanie Calmenson
Illustrations copyright © 1990 by Alan Tiegreen
All rights reserved.
No part of this book may be reproduced or utilized
in any form or by any means, electronic or mechanical,
including photocopying, recording
or by any information storage and retrieval system,
without permission in writing from the Publisher.
Inquiries should be addressed to
William Morrow and Company, Inc.,
1350 Avenue of the Americas, New York, NY 10019
First Beech Tree Edition, 1991.
Manufactured in China.

12 13 14 15 16 17 18 19 20

Library of Congress Cataloging-in-Publication Data
Miss Mary Mack and other children's street rhymes /
compiled by Joanna Cole and Stephanie
Calmenson ; illustrated by Alan Tiegreen.
p. cm.
Summary: A collection of rhymes used in street games remembered
from the compilers' childhoods and those of their friends. Includes
basic instructions for the activities.
ISBN 0-688-09749-9
1. Rhyming games—Juvenile literature. 2. Jump rope rhymes—
Juvenile literature. 3. Counting-out rhymes—Juvenile literature.
[1. Games. 2. Nursery rhymes. 3. Jump rope rhymes. 4. Counting-
out rhymes. 5. Poetry—Collections.] I. Cole, Joanna.
II. Calmenson, Stephanie. III. Tiegreen, Alan, ill.
GV1218.R58M57 1990
796.1'4—dc20 89-37266 CIP AC

CONTENTS

CHILDREN'S STREET RHYMES   7

Hand-Clapping Rhymes   9

Ball-Bouncing Rhymes   21

Counting-Out Rhymes   31

Just-for-Fun Rhymes   42

Teases and Comebacks   54

WHERE TO FIND MORE   60

INDEX OF FIRST LINES   62

CHILDREN'S STREET RHYMES

Wherever there are kids, there are rhymes. In this book you will find some favorite American street rhymes that have been recited, chanted, and sung for generations. You'll find game rhymes for hand clapping and ball bouncing, counting-out rhymes for choosing "It," rhymes to say just for fun, and, of course, those all-important teases, taunts, and comebacks.

There are many, many versions of most street rhymes. We have chosen rhymes we remember from our own childhoods, or ones told to us by friends of all ages. Some will be the same as the rhymes you know, but others will surprise you.

HAND-CLAPPING RHYMES

To do a hand-clapping rhyme, face your partner, clap your hands in a special pattern, and say or sing the rhyme. The basic pattern goes like this: clap your own hands together; clap both your hands against your partner's hands; clap your own hands again; clap your partner's right hand with your right hand; clap your own hands together; and clap your partner's left hand with your left hand.

You can make the pattern more interesting by slapping your thighs, snapping your fingers, crossing your hands over your heart, or clapping the backs of your partner's hands with the backs of yours. Then speed up the clapping and see how fast you can go!

My boyfriend's name is Jello.
He comes from Monticello.
With three fat toes
And a dimple on his nose,
And that's the way my story goes.

As I went up the apple tree,
All the apples fell on me.
Bake a pudding, bake a pie,
Did you ever tell a lie?
Yes, you did, you know you did,
You broke your mother's teapot lid.

I am a pretty little Dutch girl,
As pretty as pretty can be.
And all the boys around the block
Are crazy over me, me, me.
I L-O-V-E, love you,
All the T-I-M-E, time.
I K-I-S-S, kiss you,
Please be M-I-N-E, mine, mine, mine.

Under the bamboo, under the tree,
Big enough for you, my darling,
Big enough for me.
After we're married, happy we'll be,
Under the bamboo, under the bamboo tree.
If you'll be M-I-N-E, mine, I'll be T-H-I-N-E, thine.
And I'll L-O-V-E, love you, all the T-I-M-E, time.
You are the B-E-S-T, best, of all the R-E-S-T, rest,
And I'll L-O-V-E, love you, all the T-I-M-E, time.
Rock 'em up, sock 'em up, any old time,
Match in the gas tank, boom-boom!

Ooo-ah, wanna piece of pie,
Pie too sweet, wanna piece of meat,
Meat too tough, wanna ride a bus,
Bus too full, wanna ride a bull,
Bull too fat, want your money back,
Money too green, wanna jelly bean,
Jelly bean not cooked, wanna read a book,
Book not read, wanna go to bed.
So close your eyes and count to ten,
And if you miss, start all over again.

Oh, little playmate,
Come out and play with me.
And bring your dollies three,
Climb up my apple tree.
Slide down my rainbow,
Into my cellar door,
And we'll be jolly friends
Forevermore, more, more.

So sorry, playmate,
I cannot play with you.
My dolly has the flu,
Boo-hoo, hoo-hoo, hoo-hoo.
I've got no rainbow,
I've got no cellar door,
But we'll be jolly friends
Forevermore, more, more.

Oh, little devil,
Come out and fight with me.
And bring your pitchforks three,
Climb up my poison ivy.
Slide down my lightning,
Into my dungeon door,
And we'll be jolly enemies
Forevermore, one, two, three, four!

Oh, little devil,
I cannot fight with you.
My pitchfork caught on fire,
The flames rose higher and higher.
I have no lightning,
I have no dungeon door,
But we'll be jolly enemies
Forevermore, one, two, three, four!

Miss Lucy had a baby.
She named him Tiny Tim.
She put him in the bathtub
To see if he could swim.

He drank up all the water.
He ate up all the soap.
He tried to eat the bathtub,
But it wouldn't go down his throat.

Miss Lucy called the doctor.
Miss Lucy called the nurse.
Miss Lucy called the lady
With the alligator purse.

In walked the doctor,
In walked the nurse,
In walked the lady
With the alligator purse.

"Measles," said the doctor.
"Chicken pox," said the nurse.
"Mumps," said the lady
With the alligator purse.

"Penicillin," said the doctor.
"Aspirin," said the nurse.
"Pizza," said the lady
With the alligator purse.

A dime for the doctor,
A nickel for the nurse,
Nothing for the lady
With the alligator purse.

Out walked the doctor,
Out walked the nurse,
Out walked the lady
With the alligator purse.

The spades go tulips together,
Tie them together,
Bring back my love to me.
What am I thinking of?
I do not know.

The spades go tulips together,
Tie them together,
Bring back my love to me.
What is the meaning?

For love is the story,
The story of
Eeny, beeny,
Cha-cha cheenie,
Ooh, ah, bubble-eney,
Cha-cha-cha.
There goes Liberace.

Eeny, meeny, pasadini,
Alla, balla, boomerini,
Archie, parchie, liverarchie,
And your brother George.

Peach, plum, have a stick
Of chewing gum.
If you want the other half,
This is what you say:
Aman, aman, amandiego,
Sandiego, hocus pocus dominocus,
Sis, sis, siscumbah,
Rah, rah, rah.

My mother works in a bakery,
Yum-yum.
My father works on a garbage truck,
P.U., yum-yum.
My sister works for the phone company,
Blah-blah, P.U., yum-yum.

(On "Yum-yum," the clappers rub their stomachs; on "P.U.," they hold their noses; on "Blah-blah," they hold a "phone" to their ears.)

Miss Mary Mack, Mack, Mack,
All dressed in black, black, black,
With silver buttons, buttons, buttons,
All down her back, back, back.
She went upstairs to make her bed,
She made a mistake and bumped her head;
She went downstairs to wash the dishes,
She made a mistake and washed her wishes;
She went outside to hang her clothes,
She made a mistake and hung her nose.

Bo-bo-skee,
Watten-tatten,
Ah-ah,
Ah-ah,
Boom, boom, boom.
Eeny meeny,
Watten-tatten,
Bo-bo-skee,
Watten-tatten.
One slice,
Two slice,
Three slice,
Freeze!

(On the word "freeze," both players hold still; the
first to move or blink loses the contest.)

A sailor went to sea, sea, sea,
To see what he could see, see, see,
But all that he could see, see, see,
Was the bottom of the deep blue sea, sea, sea.

(On the last three words of each line, players stop
clapping and salute three times.)

My mommy told me, if I was goody,
That she would buy me a rubber dolly.
But someone told her I kissed a soldier,
Now she won't buy me a rubber dolly.

Have you ever, ever, ever,
In your long-legged life
Seen a long-legged sailor
Kiss his long-legged wife?
No, I never, never, never,
In my long-legged life
Saw a long-legged sailor
Kiss his long-legged wife.

I met my boyfriend at the candy store.
He bought me candy,
He bought me cake,
He brought me home
With a bellyache.
Grandma, Grandma, I feel sick.
Call the doctor, quick, quick, quick.
Doctor, Doctor, will I die?
Close your eyes and count to five.
One, two, three, four, five.
I'm alive!

BALL-BOUNCING RHYMES

When you first learn to bounce a ball, it's a challenge to bounce it even a few times without missing. But pretty soon, that's too easy. Then it's fun to add some ball-bouncing rhymes. You bounce the ball in time to the rhythm, and you do stunts as you go. You usually turn your leg over the ball on the last word in each line. For variety, you can turn your *other* leg over, bounce the ball against a wall, clap your hands, or turn your whole body around between bounces. Sometimes you have to make up part of the rhyme yourself, so your brain has to work as you bounce.

Bouncie, bouncie, ballie,
My sister's name is Paulie.
I gave her a slap,
She paid me back,
Bouncie, bouncie, ballie.

Number one, touch your tongue.
Number two, touch your shoe.
Number three, touch your knee.
Number four, touch the floor.
Number five, learn to jive.
Number six, pick up sticks.
Number seven, go to heaven.
Number eight, shut the gate.
Number nine, touch your spine.
Number ten, do it all again!

(Act out the rhyme as you bounce.)

"Hello, hello, hello, sir.
Meet me at the grocer."
"No, sir."
"Why, sir?"
"Because I have a cold, sir."
"Where did you get your cold, sir?"
"At the North Pole, sir."
"What were you doing there, sir?"
"Counting polar bears, sir."
"How many did you count, sir?"
"One, sir; two, sir; three, sir; four, sir;
five, sir; six, sir; seven, sir; eight, sir;
nine, sir; ten, sir."
"Good-bye, good-bye, good-bye, sir!
See you next July, sir."

One, two, three, alary,
I spy Mrs. Sairy
Sitting on a dictionary
Just like a green canary.

One, two, three, a nation,
I received my confirmation
On this day of declaration.
One, two, three, a nation.

One, two, three, four,
Charlie Chaplin went to war.
He taught the ladies how to dance,
And this is what he taught them.
Heel, toe, over you go,
Heel, toe, over you go;
Salute to the king,
And bow to the queen,
And turn your back
On the submarine.

"A, My Name Is Alice" is a popular alphabet rhyme. Use the names, places, and things given here, or make up your own.

Bounce the ball on each word and turn your leg over the ball only on those words that begin with the letter that starts the verse. For example, in the first verse, turn on "A," "Alice," "And," "Al," "Alabama," "And," and "apples."

A, my name is Alice,
And my husband's name is Al.
We come from Alabama,
And we sell apples.

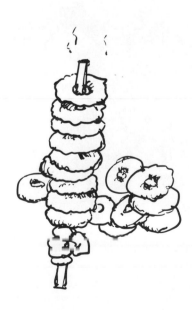

B, my name is Barbara,
And my husband's name is Bob.
We come from Boston,
And we sell beans.

C, my name is Carol,
And my husband's name is Carl.
We come from Chicago,
And we sell carts.

D, my name is Donna,
And my husband's name is Dave.
We come from Denver,
And we sell doughnuts.

E, my name is Ellen,
And my husband's name is Ed.
We come from Evanston,
And we sell eggs.

F, my name is Frances,
And my husband's name is Frank.
We come from Florida,
And we sell frankfurters.

G, my name is Gloria,
And my husband's name is Gus.
We come from Georgia,
And we sell gum.

H, my name is Harriet,
And my husband's name is Hank.
We come from Hohokus,
And we sell hoops.

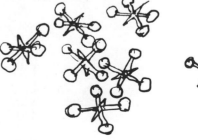

I, my name is Ida,
And my husband's name is Irv.
We come from Indiana,
And we sell ice cream.

J, my name is Janet,
And my husband's name is John.
We come from Jamaica,
And we sell jacks.   and continue through the alphabet . . .

Sam, Sam, dirty old man,
Washed his face in a frying pan,
Combed his hair with the leg of a chair,
And danced with his nose way up in the air!

Mickey Mouse, he had a house,
Clapped his hands,
Stamped his foot,
Wiggled his tail,
Sat in a pail,
Jumped out of the house.

Hippity hop to the barbershop
To buy a stick of candy.
One for you and one for me,
And one for sister Mandy.

Hello, hello, Bill.
Where are you going, Bill?
Uptown, Bill.
What for, Bill?
To pay the gas bill.
How much, Bill?
A ten-dollar bill.

For this ball-bouncing game, the player must
make up sentences in which every word begins
with the same letter of the alphabet. Here's a popular one for the letter *E:*

**Extra! Extra! Extra! Every Egyptian eats exactly
eighty-eight enormous eggs every Easter evening.**

"Names Names Names" is a ball-bouncing game for several players. One player bounces the ball three times and says:

Names of animals,
Names of animals,
Names of animals.

Then she bounces the ball to another player, who must bounce three times and name a kind of animal:

Pigs, Pigs, Pigs.

She bounces the ball to a third player, or back to the first, who must name another kind of animal:

Gorillas, Gorillas, Gorillas.

At any time, a player may change the subject by saying three times "Names of flowers" (or states, cars, movies, rock groups, or any other category she thinks of).

COUNTING-OUT RHYMES

When you are playing a game like tag or hide-and-seek, how do you pick who will be "It"? Use a counting-out rhyme.

Usually the players stand in a circle and the counter points to each person in turn for every word of the rhyme. The person on the last word goes out, and the counting starts over. Whoever is left at the end is "It."

**Monkey, monkey, bottle of pop,
On which monkey do we stop?
One, two, three,
Out goes *he*.**

Eena, meena, dippa deena,
Delia, dahlia, dominee,
Hatcha, patcha, dominatcha,
Hi, pon, tuss, *out*.

Eeny, meeny, figgledy fig,
Delia, dahlia, dominig,
Ozy, pozy, doma-nozy,
Tee, tau, tut.
Uggledy buggledy boo
Out goes *you!*

Eeny, meeny, miney, mo.
Catch a tiger by the toe.
If he hollers, let him go.
My mother says to pick this one,
And out goes Y-O-*U.*

One potato,
Two potato,
Three potato,
Four.
Five potato,
Six potato,
Seven potato,
More.

(For **"One Potato, Two Potato,"** players stand in a circle and hold out their fists. The counter taps each fist with his own, and to count himself, he taps his other fist and his mouth or chin. If your fist is tapped on the word "more," you put it behind your back. When your second fist is put behind you, you are out.)

Bumblebee, bumblebee,
Stung a man upon his knee,
Stung a pig upon his snout.
I say you are *out.*

Ocka, bocka, soda crocka,
Ocka, bocka, boo.
In comes Uncle Sam,
And out goes Y-O-*U*.

Icky, bicky, soda cricky,
Icky, bicky, boo.
Icky, bicky, here's the tricky,
Out goes *you*.

Eeny, meeny, tipsy, teeny,
Apple Jack, Paul Sweeney,
Dotchy, potchy, Don Morotchy,
O, par, dar, see,
Out goes Y-O-*U*.

Ickabocker, ickabocker, ickabocker, boo!
Ickabocker, soda cracker, out goes Y-O-*U!*

Acka, backa, soda cracka,
Acka, backa, boo.
If your daddy chews tobacco,
Out goes Y-O-*U.*

Eeny, meeny, choo cha leeny,
I buy gumbaleeny.
Achee, pachee, liverachee,
Out you *go!*

One, two, three, four, five, six, seven.
All good children go to heaven.
When they get there they will say
Johnny went the other way.

(In place of "Johnny,"
use the name of the person
who is going out.)

Intery, mintery, cutery, corn,
Apple seed and apple thorn.
Wire, briar, limber, lock,
How many geese to make a flock?
One flew east and one flew west;
One flew over the cuckoo's *nest.*

Tarzan, Tarzan, in a tree.
Tarzan fell out.

Don't give me the dishcloth wet.
Allie, Annie, Tony, Bet.
Now run out and play about
Since you've wrung the dishcloth *out.*

Once an apple met an apple.
Said the apple to the apple,
"Why the apple don't the apple
Get the apple *out* of here?"

One, two, three,
The bumblebee.
The rooster crows,
And away he *goes*.

One, two, three.
One, two, three.
Out in the middle
Of the dark blue *sea*.

One, two, three,
Mother caught a flea.
Flea died, mother cried.
Out goes *she*.

One, two, sky blue.
All out but *you*.

COUNTING OUT WITH QUESTIONS AND ANSWERS

These counting-out rhymes all ask a question. If the counter points to you on the last word of the question, you must answer. Then the counter continues the rhyme. A different person will go out, depending on the answer given. (The answers shown here are just examples. You can answer any way you like.)

Engine, engine number nine
Running on Chicago line.
If the train should jump the track,
Do you want your money back?
   "Yes."
Y-E-S spells yes and you are not *It.*

Words that are printed this way— "Yes"
—are sample answers to the questions.

All around the butter dish,
One, two, three.
If you want a pretty girl,
Just pick me.
Blow the bugles,
Beat the drums.
Tell me when your birthday comes.
   "July tenth."
J-U-L-Y. One, two, three, four, five,
six, seven, eight, nine, *ten*.

Each, peach, pear, plum.
When does your birthday come?
   "April fourth."
A-P-R-I-L. One, two, three, *four*.

As I went down the Icky Picky lane,
I met some Icky Picky people.
What color were they dressed in—
Red, white, or blue?
  "Red."
R-E-D spells *red*.

My mother and your mother
Were hanging out the clothes.
My mother gave your mother
A punch on the nose.
What color was the blood?
Shut your eyes and think.
  "Blue."
B-L-U-E spells blue, and out you *go*.

Here's your fortune, here's your fame,
Now's the time to say your name.
   "Alex."
A-L-E-X, and you are not *It*.

Old Mother Ink
Fell down the sink.
How many miles
Did she fall?
   "Three."
One, two, *three*.

The sky is blue.
How old are you?
   "Nine."
One, two, three, four, five, six, seven, eight,
nine.

JUST-FOR-FUN RHYMES

In between games, you can pass the time saying these funny rhymes. There are rhymes for walking down the street, making fun of your teacher, predicting the future, dying, going to the bathroom—you name it!

Birdie, birdie, in the sky,
Why'd you do that in my eye?
Gee, I'm glad that cows don't fly.

A horse and a flea and three blind mice
Sat on a curbstone shooting dice.
The horse he slipped and sat on the flea.
The flea said, "Whoops, there's a horse on me!"

Way down south where bananas grow,
A grasshopper stepped on an elephant's toe.
The elephant said, with tears in his eyes,
"Pick on somebody your own size."

Three, six, nine,
The rooster drank wine,
The monkey chewed tobacco
On a streetcar line.
The streetcar broke,
The monkey got choke,
And they all went to heaven
In a little rowboat.
Oh, yeah!

I'm Popeye, the sailorman.
I live in a garbage can.
I eat all the worms
And spit out the germs.
I'm Popeye, the sailorman!
Toot! Toot!

Lincoln, Lincoln, I been thinkin',
What the heck have you been drinkin'?
Was it whiskey? Was it wine?
Oh my gosh, it's turpentine!

Karen and Richie sitting in a tree,
K-I-S-S-I-N-G!
First comes love, then comes marriage,
Then comes Karen with a baby carriage.

Me no worry, me no care,
Me go marry a millionaire;
If he die, me no cry,
Me go marry another guy.

I'm Chiquita Banana, and I'm here to say,
If you want to get rid of your teacher today,
Just peel a banana, put it on the floor,
And watch your teacher slide out of the door.

No more pencils, no more books!
No more teacher's dirty looks!

Finders keepers,
Losers weepers.

I scream, you scream,
We all scream for ice cream!

I asked my mother for fifty cents
To see an elephant jump a fence.
He jumped so high, he reached the sky,
And didn't get back till the Fourth of July.

It's raining, it's pouring,
The old man is snoring;
He went to bed and bumped his head
And couldn't get up in the morning.

Rich man, poor man, beggar man, thief,
Lawyer, doctor, merchant, chief.

(This fortune-telling rhyme predicts who you'll
marry. Touch the buttons on your shirt or coat as
you say each name. When you reach the last but-
ton, that's who your husband will be.)

POOR MOM!

Step on a crack,
Break your mother's back.

Step on a line,
Break your mother's spine.

Step in a hole,
Break your mother's sugar bowl.

Step in a ditch,
Your mother's nose will itch.

How dry I am, how wet I'll be,
If I don't find the bathroom key.
I found the key, but it's too late.
I already missed my bathroom date.

Tra-la-la-boom-de-ay,
We'll take your pants away,
And while you're standing there,
We'll take your underwear!

SPELLING RHYMES

MISSISSIPPI

M, I, crooked letter, crooked letter, I,
Crooked letter, crooked letter, I,
Humpback, humpback, I.

CHICAGO

*Ch*icken in the *car*,
The car won't *go*,
And that's the way to spell
Chi-ca-go.

CONSTANTINOPLE

Can you Con,
Can you Stan,
Can you Constanti?
Can you Steeple,
Can you Stople,
Can you Constantinople?

NEW YORK

Knife and fork,
Bottle and cork,
That's the way
You spell New York.

POTATO

Put one-o,
Put two-o,
Put three-o,
Put four-o,
Put five-o,
Put six-o,
Put seven-o,
Put-eight-o.

I wish you luck, I wish you joy.
I wish you first a baby boy.
And when his hair begins to curl,
I wish you next a baby girl.
And when you put her hair in pins,
I wish you then a pair of twins.

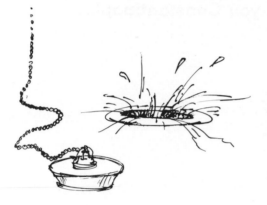

Baby, baby, in the tub.
Mama forgot to put in the plug.
Oh, what sorrow. Oh, what pain.
There goes baby down the drain!

I like myself, I think I'm grand.
I go to the movies to hold my hand.
I put my arms around my waist,
And when I get fresh, I smack my face.

Help! Murder! Police!
My wife fell down in the grease.
I laughed so hard I fell in the lard!
Help! Murder! Police!

I love my wife, I love my baby,
I love my biscuits sopped in gravy.

Did you ever think
When the hearse comes by
That you may be
The next to die?
They wrap you up
In a big white sheet,
And stick you under
Six feet deep.
The worms crawl in,
The worms crawl out,
The worms play tiddlywinks
On your snout.
Your eyes fall in,
Your teeth decay,
And that's the end
Of a beautiful day.

TEASES AND COMEBACKS

It isn't nice to tease, but no one is nice all the time. Here are some funny teasing rhymes. But don't worry—there are comebacks, too, guaranteed to put a teaser in his place.

TEASES...

Liar, liar,
Pants on fire!
Nose as long
As a telephone wire!

Roses are red,
Violets are blue.
Do you hate me
As much as I hate you?

Roses are red,
Violets are blue.
If I looked like you,
I'd join the zoo.

MORE TEASES...

Kindergarten baby,
Stick your head in gravy,
Wash it off with bubble gum,
And send it to the Navy!

I saw you in the ocean,
I saw you in the sea,
I saw you in the bathtub,
Oops! Pardon me!

I see London,
I see France.
I see someone's
Underpants.

This sidewalk is cracked
And so are you.

Cry, baby, cry,
Put your finger in your eye,
And tell your mother it wasn't I.

God made you,
But we all make mistakes.

Made you stare,
Made you stare,
Made you eat my underwear.

Made you look!
Made you look!
Made you buy
A penny book!

Happy birthday to you.
You belong in the zoo!
You look like a monkey,
And you act like one, too!

Every party needs a pooper,
That's why we invited you!
Party pooper! Party pooper!

COMEBACKS

Sticks and stones will break my bones,
But names will never harm me.

You call me this,
You call me that,
You call yourself
A dirty rat!

Twinkle, twinkle, little star,
What you say is what you are.

I wish I were a grapefruit,
And here's the reason why:
When you came to eat me,
I'd squirt you in the eye.

That's my name.
Don't wear it out.

Sha-ame, sha-ame,
Everybody knows your name.

I know *you* are,
But what am I?

I'm rubber, and you're glue.
It bounces off me, and it sticks on you.

WHERE TO FIND MORE

SOME SOURCES FOR STREET RHYMES

Abrahams, Roger D., ed. *Counting-Out Rhymes: A Dictionary*. Published for the American Folklore Society. Austin: University of Texas Press, 1980.

Delamar, Gloria T. *Children's Counting-Out Rhymes, Fingerplays, Jump-Rope and Ball-Bounce Chants, and Other Rhythms*. Jefferson, N.C.: McFarland, 1983.

Evans, Patricia. *Rimbles*. New York: Doubleday & Co., 1961.

Frankel, Lillian, and Godfrey Frankel. *101 Best Games for Girls*. New York: Sterling, 1952.

Gallagher, Rachel. *Games in the Street*. New York: Four Winds Press, 1976.

Knapp, Herbert, and Mary Knapp. *One Potato, Two Potato . . . The Secret Education of American Children*. New York: W. W. Norton, 1976.

Langstaff, John, and Carol Langstaff. *Shimmy Shimmy Coke-Ca-Pop!* New York: Doubleday & Co., 1973.

Nelson, Esther L. *Musical Games for Children of All Ages*. New York: Sterling, 1976.

Opie, Iona, and Peter Opie. *The Lore and Language of School Children*. Oxford: Clarendon Press, 1959.

Turner, Ian. *Cinderella Dressed in Yella*. New York: Taplinger Publishing Co., 1972.

Wiswell, Phil. *Kids' Games: Traditional Indoor & Outdoor Activities for Children of All Ages*. New York: Doubleday & Co., 1987.

Withers, Carl. *A Rocket in My Pocket*. New York: Holt, 1948.

Yoffie, Leah Rachel Clara. "Three Generations of Singing Games in St. Louis," *Journal of American Folklore*, vol. 60 (1947), pp. 1–51.

INDEX OF FIRST LINES

A, my name is Alice, 26
Acka, backa, soda cracka, 35
All around the butter dish, 39
As I went down the Icky Picky lane, 40
As I went up the apple tree, 10
Baby, baby, in the tub, 52
Birdie, birdie, in the sky, 42
Bo-bo-skee, 18
Bouncie, bouncie, ballie, 21
Bumblebee, bumblebee, 33
Can you Con, 51
Chicken in the car, 50
Cry, baby, cry, 56
Did you ever think, 53
Don't give me the dishcloth wet, 36
Each, peach, pear, plum, 39
Eena, meena, dippa deena, 32
Eeny, meeny, choo cha leeny, 35
Eeny, meeny, figgledy fig, 32
Eeny, meeny, miney, mo, 32
Eeny, meeny, pasadini, 16
Eeny, meeny, tipsy, teeny, 34
Engine, engine number nine, 38
Every party needs a pooper, 57
Extra! Extra! Extra! Every Egyptian eats exactly, 29
Finders keepers, 46
God made you, 56
Happy birthday to you, 57
Have you ever, ever, ever, 19
Hello, hello, Bill, 29
"Hello, hello, hello, sir, 23
Help! Murder! Police!, 53
Here's your fortune, here's your fame, 41
Hippity hop to the barbershop, 29
A horse and a flea and three blind mice, 43
How dry I am, how wet I'll be, 49
I am a pretty little Dutch girl, 10
I asked my mother for fifty cents, 47

I know you are, 59
I like myself, I think I'm grand, 52
I love my wife, I love my baby, 53
I met my boyfriend at the candy store, 20
I saw you in the ocean, 56
I scream, you scream, 46
I see London, 56
I wish I were a grapefruit, 59
I wish you luck, I wish you joy, 52
Ickabocker, ickabocker, ickabocker, boo!, 35
Icky, bicky, soda cricky, 34
I'm Chiquita Banana, and I'm here to say, 46
I'm Popeye, the sailorman, 44
I'm rubber, and you're glue, 59
Intery, mintery, cutery, corn, 36
It's raining, it's pouring, 47
Karen and Richie sitting in a tree, 45
Kindergarten baby, 56
Knife and fork, 51
Liar, liar, 55
Lincoln, Lincoln, I been thinkin', 45
M, I, crooked letter, crooked letter, I, 50
Made you look!, 57
Made you stare, 57
Me no worry, me no care, 45
Mickey Mouse, he had a house, 28
Miss Lucy had a baby, 14
Miss Mary Mack, Mack, Mack, 18
Monkey, monkey, bottle of pop, 31
My boyfriend's name is Jello, 9
My mommy told me, if I was goody, 19
My mother and your mother, 40
My mother works in a bakery, 17
Names of animals, 30
No more pencils, no more books!, 46
Number one, touch your tongue, 22
Ocka, bocka, soda crocka, 34
Oh, little devil, 13
Oh, little playmate, 12

Old Mother Ink, 41
Once an apple met an apple, 36
One potato, 33
One, two, sky blue, 37
One, two, three, / The bumblebee, 37
One, two, three, / Mother caught a flea, 37
One, two, three. / One, two, three, 37
One, two, three, a nation, 24
One, two, three, alary, 24
One, two, three, four, / Charlie Chaplin went to war, 25
One, two, three, four, five, six, seven, 35
Ooo-ah, wanna piece of pie, 11
Peach, plum, have a stick, 17
Pink, pink, 54
Put one-o, 51
Rich man, poor man, beggar man, thief, 47
Roses are red, 55
Roses are red, 55
A sailor went to sea, sea, sea, 19
Sam, Sam, dirty old man, 28
Sha-ame, sha-ame, 59
The sky is blue, 41
The spades go tulips together, 16
Step in a ditch, 48
Step in a hole, 48
Step on a crack, 48
Step on a line, 48
Sticks and stones will break my bones, 58
Talking to yourself?, 54
Tarzan, Tarzan, in a tree, 36
That's my name, 59
This sidewalk is cracked, 56
Three, six, nine, / The rooster drank wine, 44
Tra-la-la-boom-de-ay, 49
Twinkle, twinkle, little star, 58
Under the bamboo, under the tree, 11
Way down south where bananas grow, 43
You call me this, 58